Words can hardly describe my thanks and appreciation to you. You have been my source of inspiration, support, and guidance. You have taught me to be unique, determined, to believe in myself, and to always persevere. I am truly thankful and honored to have you all in my life.

My loving husband, Dr. Chimezie Nlewem

My beautiful children Chinedu, Chidera, Chiemezie, and Chigozie

My parents, Mr. Lawrence & Mrs. Ruth Jefferson thank you for all the support a daughter could want.

My little sister Teashayll Jefferson-Lee who is like a big sister to me

In memory of my brother, Rondi Jefferson

Chidera, our adventurous friend, is on a new mission today. She wants to learn and share the beautiful Igbo names for boys and girls, names that hold stories, meanings, and the rich culture of her people.

Chidera introduces herself with pride, saying,
"My name is Chidera, which means
"What God has written" in Igbo.

Chidera meets a sweet baby girl and whispers to her, "Your Igbo name can be Adaora, which means 'daughter of all.'"

Chidera makes a new friend, a playful boy, and suggests, "You could be called Chibuzo, which means 'God goes before.'"

Chidera visits her wise grandmother and asks, "What's your Igbo name, Grandma?" She replies, "I am Adiele, which means 'Let's watch and see"

Chidera gazes at the starry night sky and dreams of all the beautiful Igbo names that connect her to her culture.

Chidera realizes that names are like a gift from the past, connecting generations and reminding us of our heritage.

As Chidera waves goodbye to her friends, she knows that her journey to learn and share Igbo names has just begun. She can't wait to celebrate more names and the stories they tell.

Chidera's heart is full, and she's excited to discover more beautiful names and their meanings.

Names are just the beginning of the world of traditions and stories!

Chidera's school decides to host an Igbo Name Day celebration. Children from all backgrounds come together to learn about Igbo names and their meanings.

Your name is Ezinne which means "Good mother." Another classmate's name is Chigozie which mean "God Bless". And another classmate is Chinedu which means "God leads".

Chidera takes the stage and shares her knowledge of Igbo names with her classmates. She tells them about Adaora, Chibuzo, Adiele, and many more beautiful names.

Chidera's friends are fascinated by the rich history of Igbo names and the stories they tell. They appreciate the beauty of diversity and the importance of celebrating different cultures.

The Igbo Name Day celebration is a huge success. Children of all backgrounds come together, dance to traditional Igbo music, and celebrate the beauty of names and cultures.

Chidera's heart swells with pride and joy as she witnesses the unity and friendship that her Igbo names adventure has inspired.

Chidera knows that learning and sharing bring people closer. Through Igbo names, she has created bridges of understanding and friendship that will last a lifetime.

As Chidera waves goodbye to her friends, she knows that her journey to learn and share Igbo names will continue to touch hearts and inspire others to celebrate their own unique identities.

The end, but the beginning of a lifelong journey of unity and respect. Chidera's heart is full, and she's excited to explore more ways to bring people together through love and understanding.

Join Chidera on her next adventure as she continues to explore the beauty of language, Big culture, and the power of unity. Every adventure is a step closer to a world filled with love and harmony!

Chidera's Friends List

Adaeze female...........Means "eldest daughter of the king" in Igbo.

Akachi male & female ....Means "the hand of God" in Igbo.

Amara female ....Means "grace" in Igbo.

Chidi male & female ....Means "God exists" in Igbo

Chidike male ....Means "God is strong" in Igbo.

Chiki female & male............Means "God is greater" in Igbo.

Chima male & female ....Means "God knows" in Igbo

Chimezie male & female ....Means "God rectify" in Igbo.

Chinenye female ....Means "God is giving" in Igbo.

Chinyere.........................Means "God gave" in Igbo,

Chioma female ....Means "good God" in Igbo

Ekene male & female................Means "thanks, gratitude" in Igbo.

Ifeoma female.....................Means "good thing" in Igbo

Ijeoma female.......................Means "good journey" in Igbo.

Kelechi male & female ....Means "thank God" in Igbo.

Nididi female & male ....Means "patience" in Igbo.

Ngozi female ....Means "blessing" in Igbo.

Obinna male.................Means "heart of the father" in Igbo

Okonkwo male ....Means "boy (born on) Nkwo" in Igbo,

Nkwo being one of the four days of the Igbo week.

Onyinye female.......................Means "gift" in Igbo.

Uche male & female ....Means "wisdom, sense,

mind" in Igbo.

Zorena Nlewem is an educator who loves her Nigerian culture.
Zorena truly enjoys giving back to her community.
She is married with four children. She is originally from Virginia but currently resides in Georgia. Zorena believes that every child should have the opportunity to escape into a world of wonder through the magic of storytelling. With her books, she aims to ignite a love for reading, nurture creativity, and promote kindness and empathy among young readers.
When she's not busy dreaming up new adventures, Zorena enjoys going to the beach or traveling with her family and friends.
Join Zorena on a journey through her imaginative tales, and let the magic of her words light up your world and fill your heart with wonder and joy.

www.ingramcontent.com/pod-product-compliance
Ingram Content Group UK Ltd.
Pitfield, Milton Keynes, MK11 3LW, UK
UKHW060057060826
14089UKWH00046B/200
* 9 7 9 8 8 6 9 0 3 3 8 8 8 *